ReVeLATION
RIGhTLy DIVIDeD

Harpazo Publishing Company

ISBN: 978-0-9829954-5-7

Dr. Paul Felter

Website: BreadofLife.media

Email: DrPaul@breadoflife.media

Scripture Passages from the Public Domain King James
Bible

Contents

Introduction

The traditional view of the Book of Revelation teaches that chapters one, two, and three apply to us, the church, the Body of Christ. And everything from chapter 4 thru 22 is yet future.

Church tradition also tells us that the seven letters of chapters two and three were written to churches in Asia Minor, started by the apostle Paul, and have a present-day application to the dispensation of grace. But is that true?

Are the seven letters in chapters two and three relevant to the Body of Christ or other assemblies of believers in a different timeframe or setting? If the letters apply to us, the body of Christ, why did the Lord not deliver them through our Apostle Paul? Remember, John is an apostle to the circumcision, Israel, not the Body of Christ as clearly stated in Galatians 2:9.

"And when James, Cephas, and **John**, who seemed to be pillars, perceived the grace that was given unto me, they gave to me and Barnabas the right hands of fellowship; that we should go unto the heathen, and **they unto the circumcision**." - Gal 2:9

Why would Jesus use the Apostle John to deliver letters to Pauline churches and not the Apostle Paul?

Since John was an apostle to Israel, the circumcision, would not John be writing to those whom his apostleship dictated,

Israel, the Jews? In this writing, we will discover the proper intended audience for the book of Revelation.

The apostle Paul shows us how to properly understand any scripture, chapter or book of the Bible.

"**Study** to shew thyself approved unto God, a workman that needeth not to be ashamed, **rightly dividing the word of truth**." - 2 Timothy 2:15 KJV

I will answer three critical right division questions concerning the book of Revelation.

1. Who is speaking?

2. Who is the intended audience?

3. What is the timeframe or setting?

So, as the prophet Samuel spoke to King Saul in 1 Samuel 9:27,

"Stand thou still a while, that I may show thee the word of God."

The Revelation of Jesus Christ

"The **Revelation of Jesus Christ**, which God gave unto him, to show unto his servants' things which must **shortly come to pass**; and he sent and signified it by his angel unto his servant John:" - Revelation 1:1

The apostle John gives the book's context in verse one, "The Revelation of Jesus Christ." The revelation of Jesus Christ is not the Rapture of the Church, but the second coming of Jesus Christ at the end of the 7-year Tribulation. At the revelation of Jesus Christ, He returns to save Israel, defeat the Antichrist, conquer God's enemies and set up His Millennial Kingdom.

John declares that the events of the "revelation of Jesus Christ" must "shortly come to pass." How could John make such a statement if he was aware of the dispensation of grace, the church age, God's current program to save Gentiles which has been ongoing now for almost 2000 years?

If John wrote the Revelation in 95 A.D. as is commonly taught, he would have known that Roman legions had overrun Jerusalem, the Temple destroyed, and his people, the Jews, scattered. He would understand God's judgment was upon Israel, not the soon blessing of the restored Kingdom. Also, by that time, John would be fully aware of Paul's ministry to the Gentiles and the gospel of grace. By 95 A.D., God was saving Gentiles and building the body of Christ through the gospel of grace. He was not restoring the Kingdom to Israel as the Romans defeated Israel in 70 A.D. But there is no mention or even a hint of these facts in the book of Revelation.

So why did John say things would "shortly come to pass?"

I believe the answer lies with the probability that John wrote the Revelation soon after Jesus' ascension to heaven. An early date for writing the Revelation would answer the previous question. In the early chapters of Acts, Jews were looking for their Messiah Jesus's return to restore the Kingdom. They were unaware of the dispensation of grace as that began later in Acts chapter 9 with the conversion of Saul of Tarsus, our apostle Paul. I believe in the early writing for all the epistles of Peter, James, and John, as stated in Acts chapter 6.

"Then the twelve called the multitude of the disciples unto them, and said, It is not reason that we should **leave the word of God** and serve tables. ... But we will give ourselves continually to prayer, and to the **ministry of the word**. ... And the **word of God increased**; and the number of the disciples multiplied in Jerusalem greatly; and a great company of the priests were obedient to the faith." - Acts 6:2, 4, 7

The apostles appointed Stephen to distribute goods and serve tables. Peter and the other apostles ministered to writing the "word of God." They wrote their epistles while others saw to the needs of the widows. The "word of God increased" during that time as the gospels, Peter, James, and John's epistles were compiled and distributed to the

4

believing Jews. Remember, Peter, James, and John were apostles to the Jews, Israel. No one in the early chapters of Acts had a ministry to Gentiles.

The early writing of the Revelation solves the issues previously mentioned.

- John would not have know of the Temple's destruction nor the siege of Jerusalem by Roman legions.
- John would not be aware of the ministry of grace to the Gentiles through Paul.
- A long church age would not be on John's radar.
- John was unaware of the coming Judgment upon Israel and Jerusalem.

Chapter 1 verse 3.

"Blessed is he that readeth, and they that hear the **words of this prophecy**, and keep those things which are written therein: for the **time is at hand**." - Rev 1:3

John calls the Revelation "words of this prophecy." Prophetic scriptures pertain to Israel, and the mystery passages in Romans through Philemon, to the Body of Christ. Since the book of Revelation is a prophecy, its target audience is Israel.

John also states there is a blessing for those that "keep those things which are written therein." As we study, we will see that only those going through the 7-year Tribulation can keep the things written in the book. We, the Body of Christ, living under grace cannot.

"The time is at hand" – refers to Israel during the coming 7-year Tribulation as only during the Tribulation could anyone know the "time is at hand" because Jesus returns at the end of the 7-year Tribulation. As I write this, I cannot say that the rapture is "at hand." It could happen tomorrow or ten years from now. But Jews in the Tribulation that follow Jesus as Messiah and pay attention to prophetic events will know the approximate time of Jesus' return.

Look at it like this. In the early weeks of November, you see that Thanksgiving is approaching. You can see on the calendar the last Thursday approaching because you know the exact day of Thanksgiving. The same is true for Christmas. In December, you can see the 25th approaching. Your local news stations repeatedly tell you how many days until Christmas.

Those believers paying attention during the 7-year Tribulation will know the day of the Lord's return and see that day approaching. But the unbelieving world will be overtaken by the Day of the Lord as it comes as a thief in the night to them.

"For yourselves know perfectly that the **day of the Lord** so cometh as a thief in the night. For when they shall say, Peace and safety; then **sudden destruction cometh upon them**, as travail upon a woman with child; and **they shall not escape**. But ye, brethren, are not in darkness, that that day should overtake you as a thief." - 1 Thessalonians 5:2-4

In Revelation chapter 1, we read phrases like the following concerning Jesus Christ:

• "which is, and which was, and which is to come"

• "I am Alpha and Omega, the beginning and the ending"

• "I am Alpha and Omega, the first and the last"

• "I am the first and the last"

• "I am he that liveth, and was dead; and, behold, I am alive forevermore"

These are expressions of God used only by Jews. Paul never refers to Jesus using this type of language. They are allusions to the writing of Isaiah.

"Thus saith the LORD the King of Israel, and his redeemer the LORD of hosts; **I am the first, and I am the last**; and beside me there is no God." - Isaiah 44:6

"Hearken unto me, O Jacob and Israel, my called; I am he; **I am the first, I also am the last**." - Isaiah 48:12

The concept of God as the first and the last is an eternal truth but entirely Jewish.

Chapter 1 verse 6.

"And hath made us **kings and priests** unto God and his Father; to him be glory and dominion forever and ever. Amen." - Rev 1:6

Becoming "kings and priests" is not a concept conversant with the body of Christ. But pastors and teachers love to steal this verse. Nowhere does our apostle Paul even hint that the Body of Christ members will someday become kings and priests, neither in this life or the next. For the past 2000 years, we had no kings or priests ruling over us in the true church. Rome's false church has had many kings and priests ruling over their parishioners, but that is contrary to Paul's teachings. That's why the church of Rome mostly ignores Paul's writings.

"kings and priests" is a Jewish paradigm. Israel had many kings beginning with King Saul. Then came King David, then king Solomon. After Solomon, the realm split into the northern Kingdom of Israel and the southern Kingdom of Judah. The priesthood of Israel officially began with Arron, Moses' brother of the tribe of Levi. Levi was the tribe of priests. Kings and priests are integral functions within the Jewish national establishment. But a foreign concept to the body of Christ.

Chapter 1 verse 7.

"Behold, he cometh with clouds; and **every eye shall see him**, and **they also which pierced him**: and all kindreds of the earth shall wail because of him. Even so, Amen." - Rev 1:7

When Jesus returns at the end of the Tribulation, "every eye shall see him." That event is not the rapture of the church but the second coming. "They which pierced him" are the leaders of Israel that demanded Jesus' crucifixion. That is not a blanket reference to the nation of Israel. That could only make sense if the Book of Revelation were written shortly after the ascension of Jesus in the early chapters of Acts before Paul's conversion and the beginning of the dispensation of grace. At that time, "they which pierced him" were still alive to see the second coming of Jesus 7 years later at the end of the Tribulation. By 95 A.D., those that pierced Jesus were dead. So, how could John say that if the book was written at that late date? He couldn't.

Had the Jews accepted Stephen's testimony in Acts chapter 7, the 7-year Tribulation would have soon begun, and those that crucified Jesus would see His return. But that's not what happened. The Jews once again resisted the Holy Spirit rejecting their Messiah Jesus in Acts chapter 7. So, Israel was set aside, the fulfillment of Kingdom prophecies was postponed. God hit the pause button on Israel's prophetic kingdom program.

In the interim, God instituted the dispensation of grace to save Gentiles. He chose Saul of Tarsus to bring the doctrines and gospel of grace to lost pagans. That program is ongoing and will end at the rapture of the church. Then God will turn again to His people Israel completing their prophetic program He put on hold almost 2000 years ago.

"Come, and let us return unto the LORD: for he hath torn, and he will heal us; he hath smitten, and he will bind us up. **After two days will he revive us**: in the **third day he will raise us up**, and we shall live in His sight." - Hosea 6:1-2

A day with the Lord is as a thousand years. Two thousand years ago, Israel was "smitten." The "third day" is about to begin.

Chapter 1 verse 10 & 18.

"I was in the Spirit on the **Lord's day**, and heard behind me a great voice, as of a trumpet, ... I am he that liveth, and was dead; and, behold, I am alive for evermore, Amen; and have the keys of hell and of death." - Rev 1:10, 18

The "Lord's day" is the Day of the Lord. That day begins with the prophesied judgment of the 7-year Tribulation and continues thru the Millennial Reign. Another clue that the prophesied Tribulation and Kingdom are Israel's prophecies, not the body of Christ.

The apostle John was told by Jesus to write to the seven churches in Asia (v. 4). The traditional teaching is that these churches are Gentile churches started by the Apostle Paul, but that true? In Acts chapter 2, there are Jews from the province of Asia in Jerusalem for the feast of Pentecost.

"Parthians, and Medes, and Elamites, and the dwellers in Mesopotamia, and in Judaea, and **Cappadocia, in Pontus, and Asia**," - Acts 2:9

These Jews who believed in Jesus as Messiah were baptized and returned to their cities in Asia Minor. There they started small groups with fellow believers. These believers were not members of the Body of Christ as the apostle Paul's ministry had not yet begun in Acts chapter 2. These

10

churches, assemblies, were entirely Jewish, believing in Jesus their Messiah. They were "Little Flock" churches. Such will be the case after the Rapture of the Body of Christ. The abundance of believers in the Tribulation will be Jews as it is their time of redemption. If you are not familiar with the term "little flock," then read Luke 12:29-33. Jews that followed Jesus as Messiah during His earthly ministry and in the early chapters of Acts. They were not members of the body of Christ as they existed before the conversion of the Apostle Paul in Acts chapter nine.

John also refers to Jesus among the candlesticks, and the candlesticks are the seven churches. The apostle Paul never refers to the Body of Christ as a candlestick. In Matthew 15:5, Jesus calls Israel a candlestick and the light of the world. During the Tribulation, they will once again be the light of the world to all that desire the truth. The word "candlestick" is used 41 times in the Bible, always in the context of Israel.

Another interesting point is from verse 13.

"And amid the seven candlesticks one like unto the **Son of man**, clothed with a garment down to the foot, and girt about the paps with a golden girdle." - Rev 1:13

Why does John call Jesus the "Son of Man?" Because the Jews had a relationship with the man Jesus Christ during His earthly ministry. Jesus came to Israel as their Messiah/King offering them the kingdom. The Body of Christ has a spiritual connection with Jesus Christ which began several years after Jesus ascended to heaven. The apostle Paul never refers to Jesus as the "Son of Man" but the "Son of God." The "Son of Man" title is only for Israel.

Just from chapter one, the context is the Jews and Israel, not the Body of Christ.

Another name given to Jesus in Revelation is "Lamb." Twenty-seven times John refers to Jesus as the Lamb. Is Jesus a Lamb for the Body of Christ? No, He is the Lamb for Israel. The Lamb concept harkens back to the first Passover in Egypt, where the death angel passed over the homes with Lamb's blood smeared on the doorposts. The purpose of the "Lamb" was to save Israel, not Gentiles. The "Lamb" concept is entirely Jewish. Jesus is the Lamb of God for Israel, not Gentiles. When you read passages referring to Jesus as the Lamb, the intended audience is Israel, not the Body of Christ. Jesus is our Lord and Savior, not our Lamb or Shepherd. Israel is His sheep; we are His body.

The Seven Churches of Asia

Chapters two & three present several problematic issues for us, the church, the Body of Christ who believes in salvation by grace. They are as follows:

1. Jesus' primary concern is "works." There's no mention of grace or the gospel of grace. Works indicate these believers are under the Law of Moses as the Law is a works-based performance system from God.

2. Five of the seven letters contain judgment and condemnation. But the Body of Christ is not under any judgment or condemnation as Paul states in Romans 8:1.

"There is therefore now no condemnation to them which are in Christ Jesus, who walk not after the flesh, but after the Spirit." - Rom 8:1

3. Jesus tells the churches to repent, repent and repent. Paul never tells believers to repent but to believe and trust.

4. Each of the seven letters contains a promise and blessing to the overcomer. The overcomer concept is foreign to Paul's epistles as every member of the Body of Christ is an overcomer.

The Overcomer concept is found in the four gospels, 2nd Peter and 1st John. The Hebrew epistles also promote the Overcomer. The Overcomer is an entirely Jewish concept based on Moses's law, where performance is paramount. During the tribulation, the Overcomer resists the temptation to take the mark of the beast, holding fast to the commandments. Members of the body of Christ will never be coerced or tempted to take the "mark of the Beast." The rapture solves that issue. Therefore, the overcomer concept concerns assemblies of Jews enduring the Tribulation, not the church, the body of Christ.

5. In the gospels and Acts chapter one, Jesus spoke to Israel alone, as the church, the Body of Christ, did not yet exist. Why would Jesus address the supposed Gentile Churches in the Book of Revelation using John, since He declared that the Apostle Paul was the apostle to the

Gentiles? Remember, Jesus came to minister to the lost sheep of the house of Israel, not Gentiles (Matthew 15:24). Jesus gave the Gentile ministry to the Apostle Paul.

My purpose here is not to examine the entire Book of Revelation as all premillennialists agree that chapters 4 thru 22 are yet future. Chapters 6 thru 19 reveal the 7-year Tribulation culminating in the second coming of Jesus Christ.

Let's do a quick review of the seven churches in Revelation chapters two and three with the question in mind: who is the intended audience, the Jews or the Body of Christ?

The Seven Churches

Each of the seven letters addresses the angel of that church. Most pastors and teachers will tell you that "angel" means messenger, so the "angel" is the church's pastor. Really? If the Holy Spirit wanted to say "pastor," why didn't he say "pastor"? However, He said, "angel."

In Hebrews, we read concerning angels.

"Are they not all ministering spirits, sent forth to minister for them who shall be heirs of salvation?" - Hebrews 1:14

Angels are "ministering spirits" sent to Israel. Jews are the "heirs of salvation," as the promises came to them by Abraham. They receive that salvation at the second coming of Jesus Christ at the end of the Tribulation period. The Body of Christ has no ministering angels. We are "in Christ."

Jesus Christ is in us. We are sealed with the Holy Spirit. We do not need angels to teach or minister to us. That is the Holy Spirit's role in the Body of Christ.

The fact that these seven churches have angels over them is another clue that Israel, the Jews, are the intended audience. The timeframe is the 7-year Tribulation. The apostle Paul never mentions angels ministering to the Body of Christ.

Candlesticks represent the churches. Are candlesticks applicable to Israel or the Body of Christ? Let's look at scripture.

"And thou shalt make a **candlestick** of pure gold: of beaten work shall the **candlestick** be made: his shaft, and his branches, his bowls, his knops, and his flowers, shall be of the same." - Exodus 25:31

"The **candlestick** also for the light, and his furniture, and his lamps, with the oil for the light," - Exodus 35:14

"Ye (Israel) are the light of the world. A city (Jerusalem) that is set on an hill cannot be hid. Neither do men light a candle, and put it under a bushel, but on a **candlestick**; and it giveth light unto all that are in the house. Let your light so shine before men, that they may see your good works, and glorify your Father which is in heaven." - Matthew 5:14-16 Parenthesis mine

• "Candlesticks" as a symbolic bearer of light is entirely a Jewish concept.

• The light of the "candlestick" is the Law, good works.

• "For the **commandment is a lamp**, and the **law is light**; and reproofs of instruction are the way of life:" - Proverbs 6:23

• The Old Testament thru Acts 7 teaches faith + works of the Law, the gospel of the Kingdom, and candlesticks.

• Paul's Romans thru Philemon teach Grace through Faith, no works, no Law, no candlestick.

• Hebrews through Revelation teaches the Kingdom's gospel, everlasting gospel (faith + works of the Law), candlesticks.

• The apostle Paul never associates the Body of Christ with "candlesticks." Candlesticks bear the light of the Law. We in the body of Christ exhibit grace.

The Church of Ephesus

"Unto the angel of the church of Ephesus write; These things saith he that holdeth the seven stars in his right hand, who walketh in the midst of the seven golden candlesticks; **I know thy works**, and thy labour, and thy **patience**, and how thou canst not bear them which are evil: and thou hast tried them which say they are apostles, and are not, and hast found them liars:" - Revelation 2:1-2

Jesus commends them for their works, labor, and patience. As we have read elsewhere, works are related to Israel keeping the Law of Moses. That was the past and will be the future, Jews keeping the Law for acceptance by God and worthy of salvation. Not so with the Body of Christ as Grace, not works save us. The Jews at Ephesus also have patience. They are patiently waiting for their Messiah, Jesus Christ, who will return at the end of the Tribulation.

"Here is the **patience of the saints**: here are they that **keep the commandments** of God, and the **faith of Jesus**." - Rev 14:12

While they are patiently waiting for Jesus to return, they "keep the commandments of God." We, the Body of Christ, are not focused on keeping the commandments of God while we wait for the rapture. We walk in the Spirit and will of God. Striving to keep the commandments of the Law of Moses is entirely Jewish. Since God never gave Gentiles the Law or commandments, how could we be held accountable for something we never received?

"Nevertheless I have somewhat against thee, because thou hast left thy **first love**." - Revelation 2:4

Jesus rebukes the Jews at Ephesus for leaving their "first love." It seems they became more focused on works and less on Jesus, their Messiah. They must repent and return to their "first love," their Messiah. The Pharisees, in the gospels, kept the letter of the Law but not the Spirit. They were more concerned about their performance in building self-righteousness than their faith and love for God. The same is found in the church at Ephesus in leaving their first love. Jesus vows to remove or dissolve their church if they do not repent. If we were under that paradigm today, many churches in America would be long gone.

"Remember therefore from whence thou art fallen, and repent, and do the first works; or else I will **come unto thee quickly**, and will **remove thy candlestick** out of his place, except thou repent." - Revelation 2:5

Nowhere do we find such a burden placed upon churches during this present church age. There are churches across this nation that give lip service to Jesus while their focus is on social programs, social justice, identity politics, and many other non-Biblical issues.

"He that hath an ear, let him hear what the Spirit saith unto the churches; To him that **overcometh** will I give to eat of the **tree of life**, which is in the midst of the paradise of God." - Revelation 2:7

The promise to the Overcomer in Ephesus is to "eat of the tree of life." Eating from the tree of life brings eternal life. That applies to Israel, not the Body of Christ, as we already have eternal life through our Lord and Savior, Jesus Christ.

"Blessed are they (Israel) that **do his commandments**, that they may have right to the **tree of life** and may enter in through the gates into the city (the New Jerusalem)." - Rev 22:14 parenthesis mine

Those that eat from the tree of life must "do his commandments." Only then can they eat from the tree, giving eternal life. Jews in the Tribulation must keep the commandments. We, the Body of Christ, receive eternal life the moment we believe; no commandments or tree of life is required.

The Church of Smyrna

Something curious happens at Smyrna.

"I know thy works, and tribulation, and poverty, (but thou art rich) and I know the blasphemy of them which say they are Jews, and are not, but are the **synagogue of Satan**." - Rev 2:9

What is the synagogue of Satan? Who are those that say they are Jews but are not? Why should we in the Body of Christ care about Jews religious activities or a synagogue of Satan? We wouldn't. In the Body of Christ, there is no Jew or Gentile and no synagogue. We are one new man. But since the passage singles out Jews, this cannot refer to the Body of Christ. Another clue that these seven letters are to the Jews in the Tribulation, not the Body of Christ.

Do we, the Body of Christ, care about nefarious activities in a synagogue? No! But Jews in the Tribulation would as that is where they meet. Who are those that say they are Jews but are not? Remember the Nazi collaborators from WWII. Jews that collaborated with the Nazis, betraying fellow Jews for favor with the Reich.

That is repeated during the 7-year Tribulation. Some Jews will collaborate with the Antichrist system for favor hoping to escape death. Since they have aligned with the Antichrist, they are of the synagogue of Satan. That has nothing to do with the Body of Christ. Jesus gives a parallel prophecy in the Olivet Discourse.

"And then shall many be offended, and **shall betray one another**, and shall hate one another." - Matthew 24:10

Jews will betray Jews during the Tribulation because they are offended at Jesus, their Messiah. They also live in fear of death, so they collaborate with the enemy.

"He that hath an ear, let him hear what the Spirit saith unto the churches; He that overcometh shall not be hurt of the **second death**." - Revelation 2:11

The overcomer escapes the Great White Throne Judgment and the second death because they have been "faithful unto death." They will be resurrected at the second coming of Jesus Christ to rule and reign with Him in the Millennial Kingdom.

The Church of Pergamos

"And to the angel of the church in Pergamos write; These things saith he which hath the **sharp sword** with two edges; **I know thy works**, and where thou dwellest, even where **Satan's seat** is: and thou holdest fast my name, and hast not denied my faith, even in those days wherein Antipas was my faithful martyr, who was slain among you, where Satan dwelleth." - Revelation 2:12-13

Jesus with a "sharp sword" depicts judgment and condemnation, not Grace and Peace.

"And out of his mouth goeth a **sharp sword**, that with it he should smite the nations: and he shall rule them with a rod of iron: and he treadeth the winepress of the fierceness and wrath of Almighty God." - Rev 19:15

No one in their right mind wants to be on the receiving end of that sharp sword. That sword will be applied to a Christ-rejecting Israel and the Kingdom of the Antichrist. Jesus will use that sword when He returns at the end of the 7-year Tribulation to execute judgment and wrath.

The apostle Paul never mentions the "sharp sword" concerning the Body of Christ. Would Jesus take a sharp sword to His own Body? That's absurd; I think not. We are clothed in the righteousness of Christ; no cosmetic surgery is needed.

The believers at Pergamos are plagued by something called "Satan's seat." That is likely a reference to the Great Altar of Pergamon currently located at the Pergamon Museum in Berlin, Germany. Adolph Hitler relocated the pagan altar from Pergamon to Berlin during World War 2. The structure was a pagan altar to Zeus and Athena built during the 2nd century B.C. Is it possible that the Turkish government could demand that Germany return the altar that Hitler stole?

The believers at Pergamos have a problem with a group named the Nicolaitans.

"So hast thou also them that hold the doctrine of the Nicolaitans, which thing I hate. Repent; or else I will come unto thee quickly and will fight against them with the sword of my mouth." - Rev 2:15-16

Best guess is Nicolaitans represent a hierarchy of authoritarian leadership over believers. Jesus hates that; He wants believers to come directly to Him. No intermediary clergy is necessary. Jesus instructs those at Pergamos to repent. If they do not, He will come quickly and fight with the sword of His mouth, the Word.

That cannot apply to the Body of Christ as Jesus is not coming quickly to fight with His body. When Jesus arrives at the rapture, there is no fighting, just rejoicing that we are finally going home.

But when Jesus returns at the second coming, He comes to judge and make war. He comes to fight against His enemies, that includes the Nicolaitans. He comes to save true Israel.

The Overcomer at Pergamos will eat hidden manna and receive a white stone with a new name written on it. Paul never uses this type of language about the Body of Christ. We are not promised a new name on a white stone. That is entirely Jewish. Manna refers to Israel wandering in the wilderness being fed by God. In Isaiah, we read.

"For Zion's sake will I not hold my Peace, and for Jerusalem's sake I will not rest, until the righteousness thereof go forth as brightness, and the salvation thereof as a lamp that burneth. And the Gentiles shall see thy righteousness, and all kings thy glory: and **thou shalt be called by a new name,** which the mouth of the LORD shall name." - Isaiah 62:1-2

Just as the Lord fed Israel as they wandered in the wilderness after the Exodus from Egypt, He will protect and feed them for 1260 days, the last half of the 7-year Tribulation. John writes in Revelation chapter 12:

"And to the woman were given two wings of a great eagle, that she might fly **into the wilderness**, into her place, **where she is nourished for a time, and times, and half a time,** from the face of the serpent. ... And the dragon was wroth with the woman, and **went to make war with the remnant of her seed**, which **keep the commandments of God**, and have the **testimony of Jesus Christ**." - Revelation 12:14, 17

It's all about Israel and their Messiah.

The Church of Thyatira

"And unto the angel of the church in Thyatira write; These things saith the Son of God, who hath his eyes like unto a **flame of fire**, and his feet are like **fine brass**;" - Rev 2:18

The letter to the Jews at Thyatira opens, describing Jesus with eyes like a "flame of fire" and feet of "fine brass." This description portends judgment. When Jesus returns at the end of the Tribulation, He comes to judge and make war.

"And I saw heaven opened, and behold a white horse; and he that sat upon him was called Faithful and True, and in righteousness he doth **judge and make war**." - Rev 19:11

For the Body of Christ, any judgment due us was paid by Jesus on the cross. We are the recipients of grace, not judgment. Sure, the Holy Spirit will convict us of sin and guide us to the will of God. But grace and judgment are mutually exclusive. Grace cancels judgment. Not so for Israel during the Tribulation.

The believers at Thyatira tolerate a prophetess named Jezebel. The original Jezebel in 1st Kings was a Gentile who worshipped Baal and Ashtaroth. Her punishment was to be eaten by dogs. This prophetess in Thyatira suffers a different and unique fate.

"And I gave her space to repent of her fornication; and she repented not. Behold, I will cast her into a bed, and them that commit adultery with her into **great Tribulation**, except they repent of their deeds." - Rev 2:21-22

She and her followers, not willing to repent, are cast into "great tribulation." That is a reference to the last half of the 7-year Tribulation spoken by Jesus.

"For then shall be **great tribulation**, such as was not since the beginning of the world to this time, no, nor ever shall be." - Matthew 24:21

Revelation chapter seven speaks to those martyred during the last half of the Tribulation.

"And I said unto him, Sir, thou knowest. And he said to me, These are they which came out of **great Tribulation**, and have washed their robes, and made them white in the blood of the Lamb." - Rev 7:14

That pertains to Jews in the 7-year Tribulation. God will never cast a member of the Body of Christ into the "great tribulation."

"And I will kill her children with **death**; and all the churches shall know that I am he which searcheth the reins and hearts: and I will give unto every one of you according to your **works**." - Rev 2:23

I always found that phrase puzzling. It seems redundant to kill someone with death. Then I remembered the 4th horseman of Revelation chapter 6.

"And I looked and behold a pale horse: and **his name that sat on him was Death**, and hell followed with him. And power was given unto them over the fourth part of the earth, to kill with sword, and with hunger, and with death, and with the beasts of the earth." - Rev 6:8

The name of the pale horse rider is Death. He kills so many people during the 7-year Tribulation that Hell follows close, quickly gathering the lost dead. During the Tribulation, the horse rider named Death destroys the followers of Jezebel. Now the phrase makes sense.

Another curious passage to the believers at Thyatira refers to Satan.

"But unto you I say, and unto the rest in Thyatira, as many as have not this doctrine, and which have not known the **depths of Satan**, as they speak; I will put upon you none other burden. But that which ye have already **hold fast till I come**." - Rev 2:24-25

How does one come to know the depths of Satan? Can we, the Body of Christ, know the depths of Satan? No. Only after his removal from heaven can one understand the depths of Satan. Once here on earth, Satan unleashes his dreadful wrath because his time is short. His expulsion from heaven comes at the midpoint of the 7-year Tribulation.

"And the great dragon was cast out, that old serpent, called the Devil, and Satan, which deceiveth the whole world: he was **cast out into the earth, and his angels were cast out with him**." - Rev 12:9

The "depths of Satan" are fully manifest during the last half of the Tribulation. Another vital clue that the letters to the seven churches are for Jewish believers during the 7-year Tribulation.

Hold on to the end is the command given to believers at Thyatira.

"And he that overcometh, and keepeth my works **unto the end**, to him will I give power over the nations: And he shall rule them with a rod of iron; as the vessels of a potter shall they be broken to shivers: even as I received of my Father." - Rev 2:26-27

The Jewish believers during the Tribulation are operating under the Law of Moses. That's why the focus is on keeping the commandments and works. Those at Thyatira are to keep the works of the Lord "unto the end." Either the end of their life or the end of the Tribulation, whichever comes first.

There is a similar verse in the Olivet Discourse saying the same thing.

"But he that shall endure unto the end, the same shall be saved." - Matthew 24:13

Tribulation Jews must endure until the second coming of Jesus Christ. They must maintain their faith in Jesus and keep the commandments. Taking the mark of the beast means certain doom.

The Church of Sardis

Sardis has an intriguing verse about the thief in the night.

"Remember therefore how thou hast received and heard, and hold fast, and repent. If therefore thou shalt not watch, **I will come on thee as a thief**, and thou shalt not know what hour I will come upon thee." - Rev 3:3

Paul mentions a thief in the night in 1 Thessalonians chapter 5 concerning the Day of the Lord.

"For yourselves know perfectly that the **day of the Lord so cometh as a thief in the night**. For when they shall say, Peace and safety; then sudden destruction cometh upon them, as travail upon a woman with child; and they shall not escape. But ye, brethren, are not in darkness, that that day should overtake you as a thief." - 1Thessalonians 5:2-4

The Day of the Lord comes as a thief in the night upon the whole world. With it comes "sudden destruction," and all that dwell upon the earth will not escape because they are in darkness. Paul adds that the Body of Christ is not in darkness. The Day of the Lord will not overtake us. The Body of Christ is caught up to the Lord in the clouds before the Tribulation begins.

The "thief in the night" concept refers to the second coming of Jesus Christ. Most in the world will not be expecting His return at the end of the 7-year Tribulation.

Church of Philadelphia

"And to the angel of the church in Philadelphia write; These things saith he that is holy, he that is true, he that hath the key of David, he that openeth, and no man shutteth; and shutteth, and no man openeth;" - Rev 3:7

Notice that Jesus has the "Key of David." Jesus controls who enters the Kingdom and who does not. To some, it will be open; to others, shut. We see this portrayed in the parable of the ten virgins.

"Then shall the Kingdom of heaven be likened unto ten virgins, which took their lamps, and went forth to meet the bridegroom. And five of them were wise, and five were foolish. They that were foolish took their lamps and took no oil with them: But the wise took oil in their vessels with their lamps. While the bridegroom tarried, they all slumbered and slept." - Matthew 25:1-5

That parable is about the "kingdom of heaven." Jesus and John the Baptist spoke about the Kingdom of heaven during their ministries. That is an earthly kingdom

28

promised to Israel. The ten virgins are Jews coming to meet the bridegroom just before His return. Five came prepared with enough oil for their lamps, and five were foolish not bringing enough oil.

"And at midnight there was a cry made, Behold, the bridegroom cometh; go ye out to meet him. Then all those virgins arose, and trimmed their lamps. And the foolish said unto the wise, Give us of your oil; for our lamps are gone out. But the wise answered, saying, Not so; lest there be not enough for us and you: but **go ye rather to them that sell, and buy for yourselves**." - Matthew 25:6-9

That is where the parable gets interesting. The surprise announcement of the coming of the bridegroom finds the virgins asleep. All ten virgins arise and trim their lamps. However, the foolish virgins ran out of oil. They ask the five wise virgins for some of their oil, but they refuse. The wise virgins tell the foolish virgins to go to town. There they can buy oil from those that sell. That is the key to the parable.

The setting is the 7-year Tribulation just before Jesus' second coming. What must a person have to buy and sell?

"And he causeth all, both small and great, rich and poor, free and bond, to receive a mark in their right hand, or in their foreheads: And that **no man might buy or sell, save he that had the mark**, or the name of the beast, or the number of his name." - Rev 13:16-17

No one can buy or sell unless they have the mark of the beast. The five foolish virgins took the beast's mark so they could buy oil for their lamps.

"And while they went to buy, the bridegroom came; and they that were ready went in with him to the marriage: and the door was shut. Afterward came also the other virgins, saying, Lord, Lord, open to us. But he answered and said, Verily I say unto you, **I know you not**." - Matthew 25:10-12

The foolish virgins returned to meet the bridegroom. He had come, but the door to the marriage, the Kingdom, was shut. While they were away buying oil, the Kingdom's door was open, and the five wise virgins entered. The five foolish virgins called out to the Lord to open the door. Jesus' response is, "I know you not." The five foolish virgins forfeited their inheritance in the Kingdom by taking the mark of the beast. Their fate in the lake of fire is sure. Jesus has the key; he controls who enters.

I have heard many ridiculous attempts at explaining the parable of the ten virgins. The problem arises when one tries to apply this parable to the Body of Christ. It has nothing to do with the Body of Christ. It is all about Israel in the Tribulation. Since Jesus has the Key of David, He opens the Kingdom for some and closes the door for others. He decides who gets in and who is left out. No one having the mark of the beast will enter. The earthly Kingdom is for Israel, not the Body of Christ.

Mentioned again is the synagogue of Satan. The Jews at Philadelphia have the same problem as those at Smyrna, Antichrist collaborators.

"Behold, I will make them of the **synagogue of Satan**, which say they are Jews, and are not, but do lie;" - Rev 3:9

The following verse is supposedly a proof text for the rapture of the church.

"Because thou hast kept the word of my patience, I also will **keep thee from the hour of temptation**, which shall come upon all the world, to try them that dwell upon the earth." - Rev 3:10

Many prophecy students claim this is the rapture when the church is removed from the earth, spared from the hour of temptation. Since Israel enduring the Tribulation is the intended audience of these letters, that verse cannot refer to the Body of Christ. It refers to Jews protected by God during the last half of the Tribulation, sheltered in the wilderness for 3 ½ years.

"And the woman fled into the wilderness, where she hath a place prepared of God, that they should feed her there **a thousand two hundred and threescore days**." - Rev 12:6

God prepares a place for the remnant of Israel (the woman) in the wilderness. Many believe this to be Petra in Jordan. There the remnant is protected from Satan and his Antichrist for 1260 days, 3 ½ years. That is not the rapture, as many believe. It is the protection of the remnant of Israel, preserving them for the Kingdom.

Church of Laodicea

About six miles north of Laodicea is Hierapolis. In Roman times and today, a famous health resort noted for its hot springs. Eleven miles east of Laodicea is Colossae, well-known for its cold mountain streams. Both the hot springs of Hierapolis and the cold streams of Colossae were refreshing and helpful to residents. Nothing like a hot bath in winter or a cold glass of water in the heat of summer.

Laodicea had an aqueduct system bringing water from both locations. But by the time the water reached them, it was lukewarm. The hot water had cooled, and the cold water warmed. The waters had lost their usefulness, being tepid.

The believers in Laodicea will share the same quality. They will lose their usefulness to God during the 7-year Tribulation. Lukewarm water is not refreshing, being neither hot nor cold. Jesus will vomit these lukewarm believers out of His mouth. They are of no use to Him as they have consented to the world systems. Jesus will spew them out of His mouth into the great tribulation. This group will not enjoy the protection afforded the believers at Philadelphia.

"So then because thou art lukewarm, and neither cold nor hot, I will spew thee out of my mouth." - Rev 3:16

Proclaiming themselves to be rich and needing nothing, they boast of their self-sufficiency. The Laodiceans do not need the Lord.

"Because thou sayest, I am rich, and increased with goods, and have need of nothing; and knowest not that thou art wretched, and miserable, and poor, and blind, and naked:" - Rev 3:17

Deceived by their wealth, the Laodiceans believe they are doing well. Sound familiar? But the Lord's opinion of them is quite the opposite. Their delusion prevents them from seeing their genuinely pathetic state.

The Lord prospered them, but they began to rely on their prosperity instead of the Lord. Their soul became lean of the things of God.

Jesus instructs them to buy "gold tried in the fire." Gold is symbolic of holiness. Believers set apart for the Lord, wholly devoted to Him. The fire in this context is the 7-year Tribulation.

"I counsel thee to buy of me gold tried in the fire, that thou mayest be rich; and white raiment, that thou mayest be clothed, and that the shame of thy nakedness do not appear; and anoint thine eyes with eye salve, that thou mayest see." - Rev 3:18

They need to repent and stand for their Messiah, Jesus. Then they will feel the fiery trials that bring the gold of holiness. If they do not repent, they will be cut off (spewed out) from their Messiah and His Kingdom. Paul never uses this type of language about the Body of Christ.

The Throne Room.

"After this I looked, and, behold, a door was opened in heaven: and the first voice which I heard was as it were of a trumpet talking with me; which said, Come up hither, and I will shew thee things which must be hereafter. And immediately I was in the Spirit: and, behold, a throne was set in heaven, and one sat on the Throne." - Rev 4:1-2

Here the apostle John is caught up to heaven. Some say this is a type of the rapture of the church. However, John is an apostle to Israel, not the body of Christ, the church. Therefore, he could not be a type for the rapture as he represents the lost sheep of the house of Israel.

"And before the Throne there was a sea of glass like unto crystal: and in the midst of the Throne, and round about the Throne, were four beasts full of eyes before and behind. And the first beast was like a lion, and the second beast like a calf, and the third beast had a face as a man, and the fourth beast was like a flying eagle. And the four beasts had each of them six wings about him; and they were full of eyes within: and they rest not day and night, saying, Holy, holy, holy, Lord God Almighty, which was, and is, and is to come." - Rev 4:6-8

Before the Throne are four beasts, which appear like a lion, a calf, a man, and an eagle. This account by John is almost identical to a similar report by Ezekiel.

"As for the likeness of their faces, they four had the face of a man, and the face of a lion, on the right side: and they four had the face of an ox on the left side; they four also had the face of an eagle." - Eze 1:10

Isaiah has a similar experience before the Throne of God, seeing seraphim, each having six wings and singing praises to God. These three, Isaiah, Ezekiel, and John, are prophets and apostles to Israel, not the church, the body of Christ. They speak about prophecies concerning Israel.

The apostle Paul, when writing about his visit to heaven, said:

"How that he was caught up into paradise, and heard unspeakable words, which it is not lawful for a man to utter." - 2Co 12:4

Paul gave no details of his visit to heaven. But Isaiah, Ezekiel, and John wrote much about their experiences. That's because the Jews require signs and wonders.

"For the Jews require a sign, and the Greeks seek after wisdom:" - 1Co 1:22

How many times did the Pharisees ask Jesus for a sign? And still, they did not believe.

In chapter 5, John calls Jesus by three titles; the root of David, the lion of the tribe of Juda, and the Lamb. You don't need a Ph.D. to realize these titles are entirely Jewish. David, King of Israel. Judah, the son of Jacob, and the Patriarch of the tribe of Juda and the title of "Lamb." The Lamb title harkens back to the first Passover for Israel in Egypt. The Lamb was the sacrifice required by God to escape the death angel's visitation. The concept of the Lamb of God is also entirely Jewish. Our apostle Paul never refers to Jesus by any of these three titles as they associate with Israel, not the body of Christ. These titles for Jesus have little importance for Gentiles but are of crucial significance for Jews.

The Twenty-Four Elders

Also, in chapter 5, we read of the 24 elders. They are seated on 24 thrones and wearing crowns. That implies their work, whatever that may have been, is complete. But the big question is who are they or whom do they represent? Many say, as I once did that they represent the church, the body of Christ. But how does the number 24 associate with the church? It doesn't, as far as I can determine.

So, who could these 24 elders be? Since Revelation was written to Israel, perhaps twelve of the 24 are the patriarchs of the twelve tribes of Israel. And the other twelve could represent the twelve apostles to Israel, one for each tribe. Remember what Jesus said to them.

"And Jesus said unto them, Verily I say unto you, That ye which have followed me, in the regeneration when the Son of man shall sit in the throne of his glory, ye also shall sit upon **twelve thrones, judging the twelve tribes of Israel**." - Mat 19:28

"That ye may eat and drink at my table in my kingdom, and **sit on thrones judging the twelve tribes of Israel**." - Luk 22:30

There is the confirmation of the twelve apostles sitting on twelve thrones judging Israel. Indeed, the Patriarchs of the twelve tribes would have such an honor also. So, the 24 elders are likely the twelve Patriarchs and the twelve apostles of Israel. That is yet another clue that the book of Revelation is entirely Jewish. Oh, one more passage about the New Jerusalem.

"And had a wall great and high, and had **twelve gates**, and at the gates twelve angels, and names written thereon, which are **the names of the twelve tribes of the children of Israel**: ... And the wall of the city had **twelve foundations**, and in them the **names of the twelve apostles of the Lamb**." - Revelation 21:12, 14

The New Jerusalem bears the names of the twelve tribes of Israel and the twelve apostles of Israel. That's twenty-four!

Instead of the 24 elders somehow representative of the church, the body of Christ, they represent Israel. Twelve patriarchs and twelve apostles. Since the entire book of Revelation pertains to Israel, it only fits that the 24 elders also do.

That is one of the many passages the church of Rome had stolen from Israel after Augustine implement Replacement Theology in the 4th century A.D. The roots of Replacement Theology, the concept that the church has replaced Israel, began early in the 2nd century A.D. with the likes of Justin Martyr and Tertullian. They claimed that the church was the new spiritual Israel and we were the new people of God.

Both of these heresies, replacement theology and spiritual Israel, are still taught by many today.

Time of Jacob's Trouble Begins.

Chapter 6 the Seal Judgments.

There are six seals in chapter six as follows:

1. **The White horse rider** – a counterfeit Christ as the real Christ, the Lord Jesus returns to earth in chapter nineteen.

2. **The Red horse** – symbolic of a great war. That could be the Ezekiel 38 war.

3. **The Black horse** – famine usually follows a great war due to food shortages and rationing.

4. **The Pale horse** – his name is Death. Hell follows close behind to collect the destroyed souls left in Death's wake.

5. **Martyrs for Christ** waiting in heaven for God to take vengeance.

6. **The great day of the Lord's wrath**.

These six seals cover the entire 7-year Tribulation beginning with seal one, the coming of the Antichrist, the false Messiah to Israel, and ending with seal six, the events immediately before the second coming of Jesus Christ.

There is a vast amount of information in your Bible about the Day of the Lord. I will include a few verses here.

"And I beheld when he had opened the sixth seal, and, lo, there was a **great earthquake**; and the **sun became black** as sackcloth of hair, and the **moon became as blood**; And the **stars of heaven fell** unto the earth, even as a fig tree casteth her untimely figs, when she is shaken of a mighty wind." - Rev 6:12–13

We find a similar verse in Isaiah chapter 13.

"Behold, the day of the LORD cometh, cruel both with wrath and fierce anger, to lay the land desolate: and he shall destroy the sinners thereof out of it. For the stars of heaven and the constellations thereof shall not give their light: the **sun shall be darkened** in his going forth, and the **moon shall not cause her light to shine**." - Isa 13:9–10

Joel chapter 3 also describes the day of the Lord.

"The **sun and the moon shall be darkened**, and the stars shall withdraw their shining. The LORD also shall roar out of Zion, and utter his voice from Jerusalem; and the heavens and the earth shall shake: but the LORD will be the hope of his people, and the strength of the children of Israel." - Joe 3:15–16

Jesus, in the Olivet Discourse, likewise proclaims His second coming.

"Immediately after the tribulation of those days shall the **sun be darkened, and the moon shall not give her light**, and the **stars shall fall from heaven**, and the powers of the heavens shall be shaken: And then shall appear the sign of the Son of man in heaven: and then shall all the tribes of the earth mourn, and they shall see the Son of man coming in the clouds of heaven with power and great glory." - Mat 24:29–30

These verses, and many more, address the second coming of Jesus Christ at the end of the 7-year Tribulation. The first six seal judgments span the entire 7-year Tribulation. The trumpet and bowl judgments add details of events and activities within the seals.

My observation is that the seal and trumpet judgments span the entire seven years. But the bowl judgments of wrath span the last 3 ½ years after the Antichrist comes to complete world dominance implementing the mark and demanding control and worship of all people.

Let's continue with some more fascinating verses.

In chapter seven, God seals 144,000 Jews. 12,000 from each of the twelve tribes of Israel. Sealed by God, they preach the gospel of the Kingdom as Jesus spoke.

"And this **gospel of the kingdom** shall be preached in all the world for a witness unto all nations; and **then shall the end come**." - Mat 24:14

The gospel of the Kingdom is preached during the 7-year Tribulation as a witness to the King of Kings, Jesus Christ, soon return to set up His Kingdom.

Also, in chapter 7, there are several references to Jesus Christ as the Lamb. Again, the term "lamb" is entirely Jewish as only Jews called Jesus the Lamb of God. The apostle Paul never refers to Jesus Christ as our Lamb. We are the body of Christ, and He is our Head, not our Lamb.

Martyrs from the Great Tribulation.

"And I said unto him, Sir, thou knowest. And he said to me, These are they which came out of **great Tribulation**, and have washed their robes, and made them white in the blood of the **Lamb**." - Rev 7:14

Here again, we see two events that span the greater part of the 7-year Tribulation. The 144,000 sealed Jews witnessing for Jesus and a great company of martyrs gathered to God at the end of the seven years that came out of the Great Tribulation.

The Trumpets of Judgment

Chapter 8 brings the seven trumpet judgments:

"The first angel sounded, and there followed **hail and fire mingled with blood**, and they were cast upon the earth: and the **third part of trees was burnt up**, and all green grass was burnt up." - Rev 8:7.

The judgment God brought upon Egypt through Moses included hail and fire. The plague of Exodus chapter 9 destroyed the crops and trees of Egypt with hail. Here in Revelation, fire destroys a third of the trees and all the grass. What is the significance of destruction by thirds? I'm not sure but don't worry, we, the church, will not be on earth. We would have been raptured long before the trumpet judgments.

"And the second angel sounded, and as it were a **great mountain burning with fire** was cast into the sea: and the **third part of the sea became blood**; And the **third part of the creatures** which were in the sea, and had life, died; and the **third part of the ships** were destroyed." - Rev 8:8–9.

That could be a giant volcano such as Mt. Vesuvius or Mt. Etna exploding violently and falling into the sea, poisoning the water and killing a third of the sea life? Which sea receives this catastrophe? At this point, we do not know for sure. Would an exploding volcano create enough energy to destroy a third of the ships in the area? A massive volcanic explosion accompanied by a severe earthquake and an enormous gas release from the ocean floor could undoubtedly generate the force required for such destruction. Remember, these events are unprecedented events on a "Biblical" scale. Not your average catastrophe.

"And the third angel sounded, and there **fell a great star from heaven**, burning as it were a lamp, and it fell upon the **third part of the rivers**, and upon the fountains of waters; And the name of the star is called **Wormwood**: and the third part of the waters became wormwood; and many men died of the waters, because they were made bitter." - Rev 8:10–11 .

That is an asteroid poisoning a third of the fresh water in the region of impact, killing many people. Millions of people

42

rely on rivers like the Euphrates and the Nile for life. A poisoning of either of these rivers would bring the death of millions. Wormwood means poison. The meteor or asteroid poisons the waters.

"And the fourth angel sounded, and the third part of the **sun** was smitten, and the third part of the **moon**, and the third part of the **stars**; so as the **third part of them was darkened**, and the day shone not for a third part of it, and the night likewise." - Rev 8:12 .

The cause of these catastrophic events is unknown. But the devastation darkens the sun, the moon, and the stars clouding the atmosphere with smoke and fine particulate dust. They are blackened by a third, which is significant. The continents of North and South America are about a third of the earth's surface. What if the Yellowstone caldera exploded? That cataclysm would destroy the western Unites States and much of southwest Canada. The atmosphere would be filled with smoke and dust for months, and the USA would never recover.

The **fifth trumpet** of chapter 9 is quite astounding and bizarre. An angel opens the "bottomless pit" and releases millions of hybrid locust-scorpion creatures that sting everyone except the 144,000 who have the seal of God. These creatures cannot kill but inflict an excruciating sting so painful that the wounded will seek death. The menacing creatures persist for five months. The locust-scorpion organisms are demonic entities as they have a king named Apollyon, meaning the destroyer.

The **sixth trumpet** brings an army of two hundred million from the east. In preparation for that army to move into the Levant, the River Euphrates dries up, aiding their easy passage. A third of men die in the coming conflagration.

Understanding these events is difficult, at best. Many, such as the locust-scorpion invasion from the bottomless pit, will only be understood when it happens. Those in that day will suffer from LSD (locust-scorpion disorder). But fear not as the complete cure is only five months away, not enough time for a vaccine 😖.

Chapter 11 brings the measuring of the Temple. Presently, there is no Jewish Temple. During the early days of the 7-year Tribulation, construction of a new Temple begins as part of the agreement Israel makes with the Antichrist. Preparations for the new Temple have been underway for years. All the required artifacts have been created. Much of the structure has been prefabricated. The Sanhedrin has been selected. Even a high priest has been appointed. Also, pure red heifers are now raised in Israel in preparation for the blood sacrifice and cleansing of the Temple.

The Two Witnesses

Also, in chapter 11, the "two witnesses" come on the scene.

"And I will give power unto my **two witnesses**, and they shall prophesy a thousand two hundred and threescore days, clothed in sackcloth." - Rev 11:3.

These two witnesses have the power to stop the rain, similar to Elijah in 1st Kings chapter 17. It is my belief, based upon Old Testament similarities, that the two witnesses are Moses and Elijah. Some claim Enoch as one witness because he never died. However, the passage relating to Enoch states that he will never see death.

"By faith Enoch was translated that **he should not see death**; and was not found, because God had translated him: for before his translation he had this testimony, that he pleased God." - Heb 11:5

The two witnesses testify in Jerusalem for 1260 days or 3 ½ years. Once the Antichrist comes to total control, he has them killed. Their dead bodies lie in the street for three days. The godless celebrate their death. No longer must they listen to the truth. But just as the celebration goes viral, the two witnesses come back to life. The revelry quickly turns to great fear. I love God's sense of humor in this verse.

"And they heard a great voice from heaven saying unto them, Come up hither. And they ascended up to heaven in a cloud; and their enemies beheld them." - Rev 11:12

So much for the party spirit. But did they repent? Of course not. Only God's remnant gives Him glory.

The Seventh Trumpet, the Woman and the Antichrist

The seventh trumpet sounds announcing the imminent establishment of Christ's Kingdom on earth.

"And the seventh angel sounded; and there were great voices in heaven, saying, **The kingdoms of this world are become the kingdoms of our Lord**, and of his Christ; and he shall reign for ever and ever." - Rev 11:15

Everyone was thrilled, right? Wrong, the nations were angry. They want to be free of God to pursue their sinful desires. They love their sin, not God. To repay their anger toward God, He sends more "lightning, and voices, and thunderings, and an earthquake, and great hail." You would think by now they would get the message, but they don't. They will take their sin to the grave with them.

The events of **chapter 12** transpire at the **midpoint** of the 7-year Tribulation. A mystery lies in the opening passages of a "great wonder in heaven." A woman, "clothed with the sun," the righteousness of the Lord Jesus Christ with the "moon under her feet." Solomon wrote the following:

"Who is she that looketh forth as the morning, fair as the moon, clear as the sun, and terrible as an army with banners?" - Song 6:10.

The woman in the Song of Solomon is Israel, not the church, the body of Christ. The woman in revelation chapter 12 is also Israel, specifically a remnant that believes in Jesus Christ, the Messiah to Israel, and keeps Moses's Law.

The woman is about to give birth to the Messiah when "there appeared another wonder in heaven." A "great red dragon having seven heads and ten horns, and seven crowns upon his heads." The "great red dragon" imagery is Satan, who seeks to "devour her child as soon as it was born." Satan wants to destroy the Messiah Jesus as soon as He is born. That harkens back to the birth of Jesus at Bethlehem.

"Then Herod, when he saw that he was mocked of the wise men, was exceeding wroth, and sent forth, and **slew all the children that were in Bethlehem**, and in all the coasts thereof, **from two years old and under**, according to the time which he had diligently enquired of the wise men." - Matthew 2:16

Being a pompous tyrant, Herod was easily deceived by Satan to kill the babies in Bethlehem, hoping Jesus would be among the dead. But God is always several steps ahead of the devil. By that time, Jesus, Mary, and Joseph were safely in Egypt with the gifts of gold, frankincense, and myrrh to cover the expenses.

Satan then thought he accomplished his goal of destroying the Messiah with the crucifixion. But God the Father used that horrific occasion to secure the salvation of all that believe. The death of Jesus on the cross was a glorious victory for God. He could now save millions of Gentiles by

47

grace through simple faith that Jesus died for our sin, was buried, and rose again the third day (1st Corinthians 15:1-4).

The woman "brought forth a man child," the Lord Jesus Christ who will "rule all nations with a rod of iron" during the Millennial Kingdom. She is the remnant of Israel that believes in Jesus as the Messiah during the 7-year Tribulation. She flees from the dragon "into the wilderness," protected by God for "a thousand two hundred and threescore days," or 3 ½ years, the last half of the 7-year Tribulation.

When the situation with the woman seems resolved, "there is war in heaven." Michael and his angels battled Satan and his angels. Michael prevails, and Satan, along with his rebellious rabble, is thrown out of heaven to the earth.

"And I heard a loud voice saying in heaven, Now is come salvation, and strength, and the kingdom of our God, and the power of his Christ: **for the accuser of our brethren is cast down**, which accused them before our God day and night." - Revelation 12:10.

How many times have you heard this verse quoted about us, the body of Christ? Many times, most likely. Satan accusing the members of the church before God, but Jesus intervenes on our behalf. But this verse is not for us, the church. We are already saved; we are in Christ, Christ is in us, and the Holy Spirit seals us. Satan cannot accuse us of anything as our eternal life is secure in Christ. Satan accuses Jews before God during the 7-year Tribulation because they must endure and continue to the end of the

48

seven years for salvation. Conversely, salvation for Christians comes the moment we put our trust in the redemptive work of Christ on the cross. No accusation against us will stand as we are clothed with the righteousness of Christ.

When Satan and his angels arrive on planet earth, he persecutes "the woman which brought forth the man child." As stated previously, God protects the believing remnant "from the face of the serpent" for 3 ½ years, the last half of the 7-year Tribulation. The remnant is those "which keep the commandments of God, and have the testimony of Jesus Christ." They are Jews who keep the Law of Moses and believe that Jesus Christ is the Messiah of Israel.

In chapter 13, the beast, the Antichrist, comes to global power and control. Satan, "the dragon, gave him his power, and his seat, and great authority." No one is like the beast; who can make war with him? Great "power was given unto him to continue forty and two months," 3 ½ years. I can name one that can make war with him.

Another beast, the false prophet, rises to power and "causes the earth and them which dwell therein to worship the first beast." This false prophet does "great wonders so that he makes fire come down from heaven on the earth." He deceives the whole earth and "causes all, both small and great, rich and poor, free and bond, to receive a mark in their right hand, or their foreheads." The proverbial mark of the beast. Many have speculated about the mark of the beast. Everything from a bar code, the debit card, cards with the chip, chip implants under the skin, nano-chips, etc., have been suggested. I believe the technology is available, but the actual implementation yet future. Remember, the mark of the beast comes at the midpoint of the 7-year Tribulation. The rapture precludes Christians from exposure to the mark.

In conclusion, the Antichrist was prophesied by Daniel in chapters 9 and 11 of his writing. The apostle John prophesies of him in his epistles. Both Daniel the prophet and the apostle John minister to Israel, the Jews. They do not minister to us, the body of Christ. Also, Daniel and John are the only two people in the Bible that the Lord personally calls "my beloved." There is not a negative word spoken about either man.

The Everlasting Gospel

Chapter 14 opens with the 144,000 standing on Mt. Zion with the Lamb, Jesus Christ. Three times Jesus is called the "Lamb" concerning the 144,000. As stated earlier, they are Jews, and the context of the term "Lamb" is entirely Jewish.

An angel flies through the heavens proclaiming the "everlasting gospel." "Fear God, and give glory to him; for the hour of his judgment is come: and worship him that made heaven, and earth, and the sea, and the fountains of waters." A straightforward gospel affirming God as the creator of heaven and earth. No mention of grace or the cross of Christ. If the dispensation of grace was still in operation during Revelation chapter 14, wherein the everlasting gospel is preached by an angel, then the "everlasting gospel" would be false gospel and the angel accursed. Paul writes in Galatians:

"But though we, or an angel from heaven, preach any other gospel unto you than that which we have preached unto you, let him be accursed." - Gal 1:8

During the dispensation of grace, the church age, the only gospel for salvation is the gospel of grace. The dispensation of grace culminates at the rapture, following which the gospel of grace is no longer in operation. During the Tribulation period, salvation comes by preaching the gospel of the Kingdom and the everlasting gospel. Different gospels for different dispensations and audiences. The gospel of Grace for Gentiles, then the gospel of the Kingdom, and the everlasting gospel for the 7-year Tribulation.

Another heavenly angel cries out, "Babylon is fallen, is fallen, that great city because she made all nations drink of the wine of the wrath of her fornication." The fall of this particular "Babylon" occurs towards the end of the 7-year Tribulation. It is not a reference to Nebuchadnezzar's Babylon the Great of the 6th century B.C. This "Babylon" is the Antichrist's tyrannical New World Order global political, economic, and religious system.

Yet another angel proclaims that those taking the Antichrist's mark of the beast "shall drink of the wine of the wrath of God." Torment from God with "fire and brimstone" in the presence of the "holy angels, and the Lamb." Again, we see another reference to Jesus as the "Lamb," entirely Jewish imagery.

Those faithful during the Tribulation must patiently wait for His coming. "Here is the patience of the saints: here are they that keep the commandments of God, and the faith of Jesus." - Rev 14:12. Salvation requires patience, faith, and the keeping of Moses's Law during the Tribulation realized by the faithful at the second coming of Jesus Christ at the end of the Tribulation.

The Grim Reapers.

Wielding sharp sickles, two angels plunge their death instruments into the earth, gathering a great harvest of souls. Souls, not wheat but tares, evil people, minions of Satan, followers of Antichrist; gathered like grapes, "clusters of the vine," "fully ripe" with evil, tossed into the "great winepress of the wrath of God." And the blood flowed 200 miles, deep to the "horse bridles." These two angels with sickles bring judgment and death to the enemies of God on earth.

Chapter 15 brings a great multitude in heaven victorious "over the beast, his image, his mark, and the number of his name." These martyrs "sing the song of Moses" and the "song of the Lamb." They also call Jesus "King of saints." These three phrases are entirely Jewish. The song of Moses is for Israel, not us, the church. Jesus as the Lamb is also wholly Jewish. Jesus is the King of Israel, King of the Jews; He is not the King of the church. He is our Head.

Bowls of God's Wrath

Coming next, the seven last judgments, the seven bowls of wrath. The command goes forth in Chapter 16 to "Go your ways, and pour out the vials of the wrath of God upon the earth."

The first angel poured his bowl upon the earth. There came "a noisome and grievous sore upon the men which had the mark of the beast." The second angel poured his bowl upon the sea, which "became as the blood of a dead man," and everything in that sea died. The third angel poured his bowl upon the sources of freshwater, and "they became blood." The "angel of the waters" makes an interesting comment praising the Lord for giving them blood to drink. The reason for such action is "they have shed the blood of saints and prophets." Since the body of Christ has no prophets, this can only pertain to Israel. And Israel killed most of their prophets. The fourth angel poured out his bowl upon the sun, increasing its power to "scorch men with fire." The fifth angel poured his bowl of wrath upon the "seat of the beast, and his kingdom was full of darkness, and they gnawed their tongues for pain." Through all this, did anyone repent? No, they continually blasphemed God. The sixth angel poured his bowl upon the "great River Euphrates; and the water thereof was dried up, preparing the way of the kings of the east."

Let the great battle of Armageddon begin. Three unclean spirits go forth "unto the kings of the earth" to "gather them to the battle of that great day of God Almighty." Great armies take the stage at "a place called in the Hebrew tongue Armageddon."

The seventh angel poured his bowl upon the air. There came "thunders, lightning, a great earthquake, even greater than any before. The Lord does a topographical makeover on the earth as "every island fled away, and the mountains were not found." Great 70-pound hail falls to earth also. Can you imagine what a 70-pound block of ice falling at 130 miles per hour would do to your house and car? Utter destruction! But, fear not, we won't be here.

Mystery Babylon

Chapter 17 opens with an angel speaking with John about "the judgment of the great whore that sitteth upon many waters." This "great whore" has a name written on her forehead; "MYSTERY, BABYLON THE GREAT, THE MOTHER OF HARLOTS AND ABOMINATIONS OF THE EARTH." Back in Genesis chapter 10, we read of Nimrod gathering people and building the Tower of Babel in the land of Shinar, a flatland between the River Euphrates and the Tigris River located in what is now Iraq. But God confused the language, and the people left. Later Babylon became a magnificent nation under the reign of Nebuchadnezzar, King of Babylon. All false gods, idols, and pagan religions originated from this region, dating back to the Tower of Babel with Nimrod and his harlot wife, Semiramis. All modern false religions have their roots in Babylon and the Tower of Babel.

Some interesting facts about this "great whore" of chapter 17:

1. She sits on "many waters" – "waters" are peoples, nations, and earth regions. She has great power and influence over these people and areas.
2. "kings of the earth have committed fornication" with her – this is spiritual fornication, the worshipping of false gods and idols.
3. People of earth were "made drunk with the wine of her fornication." – Drunk with false religious experiences empowered by demons, leading to orgies, homosexuality, and other sexual and sadistic perversions.
4. The woman rides a "scarlet colored beast, full of names of blasphemy, having seven heads and ten horns." – this beast is the red dragon, Satan. The seven heads represent the seven major kingdoms Satan has controlled (Egypt, Assyria, Babylon, Media-Persia, Greece, Rome, and the Antichrist Kingdom). The ten horns are the ten kings that rise to power with the Antichrist.

5. Clothed with scarlet and purple garb, she symbolizes the royalty and power of false religions down through the ages.
6. She carries a "golden cup in her hand full of abominations and filthiness of her fornication." Many false religions use a cup in their false worship. This cup is full of horrors, scandals, perversions, and corruptions.
7. She is also "drunken with the blood of the saints and the blood of the martyrs of Jesus." Her false religious system is responsible for the martyrdom of many Jews and Christians.
8. The woman is a pagan, idolatrous religious system that rides the beast, a totalitarian political system.

Continuing with verse 18. The Beast that John saw "was, and is not, and shall ascend out of the bottomless pit, and go into perdition." That is a puzzle. We know the beast is a manifestation of Satan, so when has Satan possessed a human for his nefarious purposes? Satan possessed Judas to betray Jesus, and then Judas committed suicide. That would cover the phrase "was and is not." Satan will ascend from the bottomless pit to possess the Antichrist during the last half of the 7-year Tribulation. After that, he is bound in the bottomless pit for a thousand years. That would cover the phrase "and shall ascend out of the bottomless pit, and go into perdition," perdition being hell. Satan indwelled a human, Judas, for the betrayal of Jesus Christ. He will again possess the Antichrist attempting to prevent the Second

Coming of Jesus Christ. Judas and the Antichrist are the only two people in Scripture whom Satan personally indwelled to come against Jesus Christ. It works for me, but this is just my opinion; I am not dogmatic with it. Here are two supporting verses.

"Then entered Satan into Judas surnamed Iscariot, being of the number of the twelve." - Luke 22:3

"And the beast which I saw was like unto a leopard, and his feet were as the feet of a bear, and his mouth as the mouth of a lion: and the dragon gave him his power, and his seat, and great authority." - Rev 13:2

Let's continue with verse 10, defining the seven heads of the dragon. The seven heads are "seven mountains, on which the woman sits." Mountains in prophetic passages are kingdoms. These seven mountains are seven kingdoms. The seven heads are "seven kings: five are fallen, and one is, and the other is not yet come; and when he cometh, he must continue a short space.

These seven kingdoms have kings. Five were fallen at the time John wrote the Revelation.

1. Egypt – Pharaoh
2. Assyria – Sennacherib
3. Babylon – Nebuchadnezzar
4. Media-Persia – Cyrus?
5. Greece – Alexander the Great

One is in power during John's life.

6. Rome – Nero

One yet to come,

7. New World Order – 10 kings

"And the beast that was, and is not, even he is the eighth, and is of the seven, and goeth into perdition."

8. The Antichrist takes over the New World Order, defeating 3 of the ten kings.

Verse 18.

"And the woman which thou sawest is that great city, which reigneth over the kings of the earth." - Rev 17:18

The woman is a "great city," a center of false religion. What city might that be during the Tribulation? Time will tell. Will ancient Babylon be rebuilt? Some believe the rebuilding of Babylon necessary to fulfill prophecy. I do not hold to that position. The Last Days Babylon is a Mystery, ancient Babylon in a new, modern form. Same old Babylonian paganism with a new façade, a new world order for the 21st century.

The saga of Babylon continues in chapter 18. Another angel shouts a declaration about Babylon. "Babylon the great is fallen, is fallen, and is become the habitation of devils, and the hold of every foul spirit, and a cage of every unclean and hateful bird." Notice this proclamation is for "Babylon the great," that would be ancient Babylon. The ancient Babylon site is now a UNESCO World Heritage site of archeological ruins, including a modern palace built by Saddam Hussein.

In the end-times, Babylon is the Antichrist system of power. It is called Babylon due to the similarities of religious and political corruption it shares with ancient Babylon. We know this is true because the Babylon of chapter 17 is a "Mystery," "Mystery, Babylon the Great." The mystery is that ancient Babylon the Great has revived as the Antichrist's New World Order Babylon during the 7-year Tribulation.

As the second coming of Jesus Christ is near in chapter 18, the Lord calls His people.

"And I heard another voice from heaven, saying, Come out of her, my people, that ye be not partakers of her sins, and that ye receive not of her plagues." - Revelation 18:4

God's people, the Jews, are commanded to flee the Antichrist system. As it was in Nazi Germany, many Jews will feel trapped in the Antichrist System. The Lord commands them to escape the system before its destruction.

"How much she hath glorified herself, and lived deliciously, so much torment and sorrow give her: for she saith in her heart, I sit a queen, and am no widow, and shall see no sorrow. Therefore shall her plagues come in one day, death, and mourning, and famine; and she shall be utterly burned with fire: for strong is the Lord God who judgeth her." - Revelation 18:7-8

The leaders of the world's religions have always glorified themselves and lived "deliciously." Many did not flaunt their glory in public. They feigned humility to fool the naïve public. But privately, they enjoyed the best the world has to offer. This particular queen, the new world order religious system, managed by the false prophet of chapter 13, will never be a widow, or so she thinks. Her marriage to the beast political system is a match made in hell and is so glorious and magnificent it will last forever.

But God has a different outcome in mind. He will give her "torment and sorrow" in place of her glory. The plague God releases on her comes in one day. Death, mourning, famine, and fire will utterly destroy her. Her presence, erased from the face of the earth.

"And the kings of the earth, who have committed fornication and lived deliciously with her, shall bewail her, and lament for her, when they shall see the smoke of her burning, Standing afar off for fear of her torment, saying, Alas, alas, that great city Babylon, that mighty city! for in one hour is thy judgment come." - Revelation 18:9–10

The merchants of the earth who supplied the false religious system with costly, extravagant goods weep and mourn her destruction as they watch from afar. The "smoke of her burning" rises into the sky, heralding the loss of a massive market for the finer things of earthly life. Her judgment comes in "one hour." A nuclear weapon could bring such sudden destruction sending a vast mushroom cloud miles into the atmosphere seen for a hundred miles.

Mystery Babylon imported just about everything but sand.

"The merchandise of gold, and silver, and precious stones, and of pearls, and fine linen, and purple, and silk, and scarlet, and all thyine wood, and all manner vessels of ivory,

60

and all manner vessels of most precious wood, and brass, and iron, and marble, And cinnamon, and odours, and ointments, and frankincense, and wine, and oil, and fine flour, and wheat, and beasts, and sheep, and horses, and chariots, and slaves, and souls of men. And the fruits that thy soul lusted after are departed from thee, and all things which were dainty and goodly are departed from thee, and thou shalt find them no more at all." - Revelation 18:12–14

She imported everything from soup to nuts, even the "souls of men," most likely a reference to slaves. There are several countries of the world in dry, desert regions that import everything except oil. Notice that energy-related products are not on the list.

"And saying, Alas, alas, that great city, that was clothed in fine linen, and purple, and scarlet, and decked with gold, and precious stones, and pearls! For in one hour so great riches is come to nought. And every shipmaster, and all the company in ships, and sailors, and as many as trade by sea, stood afar off, And cried when they saw the smoke of her burning, saying, What city is like unto this great city!" - Revelation 18:16–18

The destruction of this city is a huge event and affects many people both on land and sea. Two centers of false religions that could play a role in the Tribulation are Rome and Mecca. Both are shipping ports near large seas, making their destruction visible from merchant vessels. That might also be the new city of Neom under construction in Saudi Arabia on the Red Sea. Time will tell. But no worries, mate, the church will not be here.

Here is a curious passage.

"And they cast dust on their heads, and cried, weeping and wailing, saying, Alas, alas, that great city, wherein were made rich all that had ships in the sea by reason of her costliness! for in one hour is she made desolate." - Revelation 18:19

Casting dust on one's Head is a Middle Eastern practice mourning a tragic event—yet another clue signaling the focal point of the woman riding the beast in the Middle East. We already know from an overall view that Israel and Jerusalem are the center of end times prophecy, not Europe or America. Europe may have a role, but America is nowhere in Bible prophecy.

Rejoice in Heaven

The scene changes in chapter 19 from Mystery Babylon to heavenly places.

"And after these things I heard a great voice of much people in heaven, saying, Alleluia; Salvation, and glory, and honour, and power, unto the Lord our God: For true and righteous are his judgments: for he hath judged the great whore, which did corrupt the earth with her fornication, and hath avenged the blood of his servants at her hand. And again they said, Alleluia. And her smoke rose up for ever and ever." - Revelation 19:1–3

A great crowd of people sing and rejoice in heaven at the judgment of God against the "great whore," the woman destroyed in the previous chapter. Over the millennia, she killed God's saints and prophets. She was worthy of God's wrath. The smoke of her destruction rises forever and ever as a reminder of God's final judgment on false Satanic religions.

The praise and worship service continues in heaven with a profound announcement, the marriage of the Lamb.

"Let us be glad and rejoice, and give honor to him: for the marriage of the Lamb is come, and his wife hath made herself ready. And to her was granted that she should be arrayed in fine linen, clean and white: for the fine linen is the righteousness of saints. And he saith unto me, Write, Blessed are they which are called unto the marriage supper of the Lamb. And he saith unto me, These are the true sayings of God." - Revelation 19:7-9

Let's unpack this passage carefully. Beginning with the quote, "the marriage of the Lamb is come, and his wife hath made herself ready." We know the Lamb is Jesus Christ. He is getting married. But notice that "his wife" has made herself ready for the marriage. Why does it read "wife" and not "bride?"

We, the church, have been told for all our Christian experience that we are the "bride of Christ." I believed that even though I could not find any scriptures to support the claim. The term "bride of Christ" is nowhere found in your King James Bible and certainly never used by our apostle

Paul. Paul declares we are the "body of Christ," not the bride.

But has God been married before? Yes, He has. Isaiah and Jeremiah tell us.

"For thy Maker is **thine husband**; the LORD of hosts is his name; and thy Redeemer the Holy One of Israel; The God of the whole earth shall he be called." - Isa 54:5

Isaiah tells us that the Lord of hosts, the Redeemer, the Holy One of Israel, the God of the whole earth, is the husband of Israel. Without question, this verse's subject is the one True God, and the object is Israel. God is the husband of Israel.

Jeremiah repeats the declaration.

"Not according to the covenant that I made with their fathers in the day that I took them by the hand to bring them out of the land of Egypt; which my covenant they brake, although **I was an husband unto them**, saith the LORD:" - Jer 31:32

Here again, there is no doubt that the Lord God is the husband of Israel. Notice these verses are declarations, not metaphors or similes. Isaiah and Jeremiah are not using the husband concept as an allegory or type but as a pronouncement.

To prove this point, Jeremiah writes:

"And I saw, when for all the causes whereby backsliding Israel committed adultery I had put her away, and given her

64

a **bill of divorce**; yet her treacherous sister Judah feared not, but went and played the harlot also." - Jer 3:8

Here the Lord God gives Israel and Judah a "bill of divorce" for adultery, spiritual fornication with idols, and false gods. That presents an interesting situation. As long as Israel lives, God cannot marry another as that would be adultery. God has made promises and prophecies concerning Israel and their restored Kingdom. So, the Lord must remarry Israel to be faithful and true to His word and name. That is what He does at the second coming.

In Revelation 19:7-9, Jesus is called the "Lamb." As previously noted, the term "Lamb" is entirely Jewish as Jesus is the Jewish Messiah/King coming to save and redeem Israel. Israel is the bride/wife of the Lord as they are whom He previously declared Himself a husband.

Nowhere does our apostle Paul picture the body of Christ dressed in clean, white linen or fine linen. However, many times in the Old Testament and here in Revelation, those terms portend to Israel.

There are two additional verses from the New Testament that add clarity to the issue.

"And Jesus said unto them, Can the children of the bridechamber mourn, as long as the **bridegroom** is with them? but the days will come, when the **bridegroom** shall be taken from them, and then shall they fast." - Matthew 9:15

"He that hath the **bride** is the **bridegroom**: but the **friend of the bridegroom**, which standeth and heareth him, rejoiceth greatly because of the bridegroom's voice: this my joy therefore is fulfilled." - John 3:29

In Matthew, the bridechamber's children are Israel, whom Jesus ministered to in the gospels. After the betrayal and crucifixion of the bridegroom, then they can mourn and fast.

The passage from John chapter 3 pertains to John the Baptist, the bridegroom friend rejoicing upon hearing the voice of the bridegroom Jesus, who also has the bride, Israel.

The true bride of Christ is not the church but Israel. The marriage takes place at Jesus' second coming at the end of the Tribulation.

The King Cometh

"And I saw heaven opened, and behold a white horse; and he that sat upon him was called Faithful and True, and in righteousness he doth judge and make war. His eyes were as a flame of fire, and on his Head were many crowns; and he had a name written, that no man knew, but he himself." - Revelation 19:11-12

In chapter 6, we saw a white horse rider come forth imitating the true King of Kings, Jesus Christ. Now comes the true King of Kings, Lord of Lords, the Son of God, the Faithful and True. He comes in righteousness, to judge Israel and to make war with His enemies. With His coming, we have reached the end of the 7-year Tribulation. His eyes as flames of fire portend righteousness and judgment.

"And he was clothed with a vesture dipped in blood: and his name is called The **Word of God**. And the **armies which were in heaven** followed him upon white horses, clothed in fine linen, white and clean." - Revelation 19:13-14

Jesus' robe "dipped in blood" indicates the coming battles as described in Isaiah chapter 63.

"Who is this that cometh from Edom, with **dyed garments** from Bozrah? this that is glorious in his apparel, travelling in the greatness of his strength? I that speak in righteousness, mighty to save. Wherefore art thou **red in thine apparel**, and thy garments like him that treadeth in the winefat? I have trodden the winepress alone; and of the people there was none with me: for I will tread them in mine anger, and trample them in my fury; and **their blood shall be sprinkled upon my garments**, and I will stain all my raiment. For the day of vengeance is in mine heart, and the year of my redeemed is come." - Isaiah 63:1-4

Wow, what a passage. Jesus is coming to fight His enemies. Glorious, powerful, and righteous, mighty to save His people Israel. His garments stained red with His enemies' blood as clusters of grapes tread in the winepress of His wrath. The long-awaited day of the Lord's vengeance has come and the year of His redeemed, Israel.

The armies of heaven come with Jesus to the earth. Church tradition tells us that we, the church, are returning with Jesus Christ to rule and reign with Him in the Millennial Kingdom. But what do the scriptures say?

"When the Son of man shall come in his glory, and all the **holy angels with him**, then shall he sit upon the throne of his glory:" - Matthew 25:31

Jesus said that when He returns to sit upon His Throne of glory in the Kingdom, He is coming with His holy angels. We in the church might be many things, but we are not holy angels. The armies of heaven are the holy angels that return with Jesus at the second coming, not the church.

But Jude states that the Lord returns with His saints.

"And Enoch also, the seventh from Adam, prophesied of these, saying, Behold, the Lord cometh with ten thousands of his saints," - Jude 1:14

Saints can refer to angels or believers. The word means "holy ones."

Let's look at another passage.

"And then shall appear the sign of the Son of man in heaven: and then shall all the tribes of the earth mourn, and they shall see the Son of man coming in the clouds of heaven with power and great glory. And he shall send his **angels** with a great sound of a trumpet, and they shall gather together his elect from the four winds, from one end of heaven to the other." - Matthew 24:30–31

68

The Lord returns, sending his angels to gather "his elect," Israel from the four corners of the earth back to Jerusalem.

"And out of his mouth goeth a sharp sword, that with it he should smite the nations: and he shall rule them with a rod of iron: and he treadeth the winepress of the fierceness and wrath of Almighty God. And he hath on his vesture and on his thigh a name written, KING OF KINGS, AND LORD OF LORDS." - Revelation 19:15–16

The sharp sword is the word of God. His word has power, and with that power, He will smite the nations. Those in rebellion against the Lord Jesus will feel the mighty sting of that sword and the crushing blow of the iron rod. Wrath and vengeance are the order of the day. It's been a long time coming, but Jesus will finally set things straight in this world.

"And I saw an angel standing in the sun; and he cried with a loud voice, saying to all the **fowls that fly** in the midst of heaven, Come and gather yourselves together unto the **supper of the great God**; That ye may eat the flesh of kings, and the flesh of captains, and the flesh of mighty men, and the flesh of horses, and of them that sit on them, and the flesh of all men, both free and bond, both small and great." - Revelation 19:17–18

The Lord prepares a special feast for the fowls of the air, a great supper. A similar passage is found in Ezekiel.

"And, thou son of man, thus saith the Lord GOD; Speak unto every feathered fowl, and to every beast of the field, Assemble yourselves, and come; gather yourselves on every side to my sacrifice that I do sacrifice for you, even a great sacrifice upon the mountains of Israel, that ye may eat flesh, and drink blood. Ye shall eat the flesh of the mighty, and drink the blood of the princes of the earth, of rams, of lambs, and of goats, of bullocks, all of them fatlings of Bashan. And ye shall eat fat till ye be full, and drink blood till ye be drunken, of my sacrifice which I have sacrificed for you. Thus ye shall be filled at my table with horses and chariots, with mighty men, and with all men of war, saith the Lord GOD." - Ezekiel 39:17-20

These verses are quite graphic. A massive slaughter of God's enemies follows Jesus' second coming. Blood flow to the horses' bridles.

"And I saw the beast, and the kings of the earth, and their armies, gathered together to make war against him that sat on the horse, and against his army." - Revelation 19:19

This battle of Armageddon is not to conquer a region or country on earth. The armies of mankind are gathering to fight against the white horse rider, Jesus Christ. Satan loves his Kingdom of evil and will do everything he can to stop Jesus from returning to earth. But his efforts are futile. The Lord's victory is swift and complete.

"And the beast was taken, and with him the false prophet that wrought miracles before him, with which he deceived them that had received the mark of the beast, and them that worshipped his image. These both were cast alive into a lake of fire burning with brimstone. And the remnant were slain with the sword of him that sat upon the horse, which sword proceeded out of his mouth: and all the fowls were filled with their flesh." - Revelation 19:20–21

The defeat of the Antichrist and the false prophet is almost immediate. Making war against Jesus Christ and His holy angels is pure folly; they never stood a chance at victory. Quickly collected by the heavenly host, they are cast alive into the lake of fire, where they will remain for all eternity. No trial, no jury, no appeals, only pure justice from the Judge of the earth. I find it interesting that for the entire Millennial Reign of Christ, the beast and the false prophet are the only two residents in the lake of fire. Are they weeping in each other's tears or at each other's throats?

The Millennial Kingdom

"And I saw an angel come down from heaven, having the key of the bottomless pit and a great chain in his hand. And he laid hold on the dragon, that old serpent, which is the Devil, and Satan, and bound him a thousand years, And cast him into the bottomless pit, and shut him up, and set a seal upon him, that he should deceive the nations no more, till the thousand years should be fulfilled: and after that he must be loosed a little season." - Revelation 20:1–3

The first order of business in preparation for the Kingdom is the disposal of the dragon, Satan. An angel binds Satan with a "great chain" and locks him in the "bottomless pit" for a thousand years. Why is Satan not thrown into the lake of fire along with the beast and false prophet? Because God is not finished with him just yet. God has one more task for the dragon to perform.

"And I saw **thrones**, and they sat upon them, and **judgment** was given unto them: and I saw the souls of them that were beheaded for the witness of Jesus, and for the word of God, and which had not worshipped the beast, neither his image, neither had received his mark upon their foreheads, or in their hands; and they lived and reigned with Christ a thousand years." - Revelation 20:4

This passage is reminiscent of an excerpt from Daniel chapter 7.

"I beheld till thrones were set, and the Ancient of days did sit: his raiment was white as snow, and the hair of his head like pure wool; his throne was flames of fire, and its wheels burning fire. A stream of fire issued and came forth from before him; thousand thousands ministered unto him, and ten thousand times ten thousand stood before him: the judgment was set, and the books were opened." - Daniel 7:9–10 DBY

In Daniel and Revelation, the judgment happens at the end of the Antichrist's reign at the second coming of Jesus Christ. Thrones of judgment are set upon the earth to judge Israel and a Christ-rejecting world.

1. The Lord Jesus Christ judges the ungodly sending them to hell to await the Great White Throne Judgment.

"And Enoch also, the seventh from Adam, prophesied of these, saying, Behold, **the Lord cometh with ten thousands of his saints**, To **execute judgment upon all**, and to convince all that are ungodly among them of all their ungodly deeds which they have ungodly committed, and of all their hard speeches which ungodly sinners have spoken against him." - Jude 1:14–15

The long-awaited judgment from the Lord finally comes to earth. The wheat and tares parable foretold such a time.

"Another parable put he forth unto them, saying, The **kingdom of heaven** is likened unto a man which sowed good seed in his field: But while men slept, his enemy came and sowed **tares** among the **wheat**, and went his way. But when the blade was sprung up, and brought forth fruit, then appeared the tares also. So the servants of the householder came and said unto him, Sir, didst not thou sow good seed in thy field? from whence then hath it tares? He said unto them, An **enemy** hath done this. The servants said unto him, Wilt thou then that we go and gather them up? But he said, Nay; lest while ye gather up the tares, ye root up also the wheat with them. **Let both grow together until the harvest**: and in the time of harvest I will say to the **reapers, Gather ye together first the tares, and bind them in bundles to burn them: but gather the wheat into my barn.**" - Matthew 13:24–30

The parable depicts an event immediately preceding the inauguration of the kingdom of heaven, the Millennial Reign of Christ. The time of harvest arrives but sown among the wheat are tares. They grew together before the harvest, but now the grain is ripe and must be gathered into the barn. The owner, the Lord, sends the reapers to gather the tares first, binding them for the fire. We read about the reapers earlier in Revelation chapter 14. There the reapers gathered clusters of grapes, casting them into the winepress of God's wrath. Here the reapers gather bundles of tares, throwing them into the fire of hell: same concept, different crop. The tares are ungodly sinners in rebellion against God during the Tribulation. Their removal from the earth leaves the wheat, the godly, to enter the kingdom.

The sheep and goat judgment is synonymous with the wheat and tares

"When the Son of man shall **come in his glory**, and all the **holy angels** with him, then shall he sit upon the throne of his glory: And before him shall be gathered **all nations**: and he shall separate them one from another, as a shepherd divideth his **sheep from the goats**: And he shall set the **sheep on his right hand, but the goats on the left**. Then shall the King say unto them on his **right hand**, Come, ye blessed of my Father, **inherit the kingdom** prepared for you from the foundation of the world: ... Then shall he say also unto them on the **left hand, Depart from me, ye cursed**, into everlasting fire, prepared for the devil and his angels:" - Matthew 25:31–34, 41

Just as the wheat and tares' judgment separated the godly from the ungodly, the sheep and goat judgment does likewise. The sheep enter the kingdom, but the goats hear those terrible words, "depart from me, ye cursed." They are taken away, just like the tares, to everlasting fire, hell.

Jesus referred to that in Matthew 24.

"But as the **days of Noe were**, so shall also the **coming of the Son of man be**. For as in the days that were before the flood they were eating and drinking, marrying and giving in marriage, until the day that Noe entered into the ark, And knew not until the **flood came, and took them all away**; so shall also the coming of the Son of man be. Then shall two be in the field; the **one shall be taken**, and the **other left**. Two women shall be grinding at the mill; the **one shall be taken, and the other left**." - Matthew 24:37–41

Many Christians are confused about this passage, thinking that "one shall be taken, and the other left" is the rapture of the church. The truth is just the opposite. Just as those "taken" in Noah's flood were ungodly, those taken at the second coming are also ungodly, the tares, the grapes of wrath. The fires of hell await those "taken." The Kingdom of Jesus Christ awaits those "left." The "sheep," the "wheat," and those "left" enter the Millennial Kingdom. The "goats," the "tares," and those "taken," enter hell awaiting the Great White Throne judgment and the lake of fire.

Another often misquoted and misapplied passage from Matthew chapter 7.

"**Not every one** that saith unto me, Lord, Lord, shall enter into the **kingdom of heaven**; but he that doeth the will of my Father which is in heaven. Many will say to me in that day, Lord, Lord, have we not prophesied in thy name? and in thy name have cast out devils? and in thy name done many wonderful works? And then will I profess unto them, **I never knew you: depart from me, ye that work iniquity**." - Matthew 7:21-23

Frequently this passage is erroneously applied to the church, the body of Christ. The people in the story are shocked at being denied entry into the "kingdom of heaven," the Millennial Kingdom of Jesus Christ. In "that day," they appear before the Lord in judgment. Making their claim for entry by their abundance of good works, Jesus proclaims, "**I never knew you: depart from me, ye that work iniquity.**" How could they have done so many good works and yet be denied the kingdom? Perhaps they took the mark of the beast nullifying their previous efforts.

The reason why this cannot apply to the body of Christ today is that we are not looking for the kingdom of heaven, the earthly kingdom of Christ, but the rapture which moves us to heavenly places. Also, we are not saved or justified by good works. Our salvation is by grace through faith and not of works.

Many scriptures portend the second coming of Jesus Christ and His subsequent judgment of Israel and the Gentile world. I have covered several here in support of His judgment found in Revelation chapter 20 verse 4. Also, note that those martyred for Jesus during the Tribulation will rule and reign with Jesus for the thousand years.

The First Resurrection

"But the rest of the dead lived not again until the thousand years were finished. This is the first resurrection. Blessed and holy is he that hath part in the first resurrection: on such the second death hath no power, but they shall be priests of God and of Christ, and shall reign with him a thousand years." - Revelation 20:5-6

Another passage with which many pastors, teachers, and laypeople struggle. Even so-called prophecy experts can't seem to get this right. They continually include the church and the rapture in the "first resurrection," thereby causing confusion and error.

The "first resurrection" is a prophesied event shortly after the second coming of Jesus Christ after Jesus destroys all the enemies of God and Israel.

"For I know that my redeemer liveth, and that he shall stand at the latter day upon the earth: And though after my skin worms destroy this body, yet in my flesh shall I see God:" - Job 19:25-26

That is perhaps the oldest passage depicting the resurrection. Job lived around Abraham's time, so the resurrection familiarity predates the Abrahamic and Mosaic covenants.

King David knew of the resurrection.

"For thou wilt not leave my soul in hell; neither wilt thou suffer thine Holy One to see corruption." - Psalm 16:10

God would not leave David in the underworld and will not leave the "Holy One" in the grave to see the body's corruption. God would raise them both from the grave. Jesus after three days and King David at the "first resurrection," after the second coming of Jesus Christ.

Hosea understood the resurrection.

"Come, and let us return unto the LORD: for he hath torn, and he will heal us; he hath smitten, and he will bind us up. After two days will he revive us: in the third day he will raise us up, and we shall live in his sight." - Hosea 6:1–2

A day with the Lord is as a thousand years. Jesus rose on the third day. Israel will rise on the third Millennia.

I John's gospel, we read.

"Verily, verily, I say unto you, The hour is coming, and now is, when **the dead shall hear the voice of the Son of God**: and they that hear **shall live**. ... Marvel not at this: for the hour is coming, in the which all that are in the graves shall hear his voice, And shall come forth; they that have done **good, unto the resurrection of life**; and they that have done **evil, unto the resurrection of damnation**." - John 5:25, 28–29

In a later encounter with Martha, Jesus said.

"Jesus saith unto her, **Thy brother shall rise again**. Martha saith unto him, I know that he shall rise again in the

resurrection at the last day. Jesus said unto her, **I am the resurrection, and the life**: he that believeth in me, though he were dead, yet shall he live:" - John 11:23–25

This verse sets the resurrection timing as did Revelation 20 verse 5, the "last day," the second coming of Jesus Christ at the end of the Tribulation. The "first resurrection" is the prophesied resurrection for Israel. From Adam through the Tribulation martyrs, all the Old Testament saints resurrect from the dead at Jesus' second coming. He is the resurrection and the life.

The rapture is not part of the "first resurrection" as it is not part of Bible prophecy. It was a mystery hid in God, as were all things of the dispensation of grace.

"But we speak the **wisdom of God in a mystery**, even the **hidden wisdom**, which God ordained before the world unto our glory:" - 1 Corinthians 2:7

"Having made known unto us the **mystery** of his will, according to his good pleasure which he hath purposed in himself:" - Ephesians 1:9

"**How that by revelation he made known unto me the mystery**; (as I wrote afore in few words, ... And to make all men see what is the **fellowship of the mystery**, which from the beginning of the world hath been hid in God, who created all things by Jesus Christ:" - Ephesians 3:3, 9

"This is a **great mystery**: but I speak concerning Christ and the church." - Ephesians 5:32

"And for me, that utterance may be given unto me, that I may open my mouth boldly, to make known the **mystery of the gospel**," - Ephesians 6:19

"Even the **mystery which hath been hid from ages** and from generations, but now is made manifest to his saints: To whom God would make known what is the riches of the glory of this **mystery among the Gentiles**; which is **Christ in you, the hope of glory**:" - Colossians 1:26–27

The rapture of the church is part of the Mystery.

"Behold, I shew you a **mystery**; We shall not all sleep, but we shall all be changed, In a moment, in the twinkling of an eye, at the last trump: for the trumpet shall sound, and the dead shall be raised incorruptible, and we shall be changed." - 1 Corinthians 15:51–52

Jesus coming in the air at the Damascus' road to save Saul of Tarsus was an unprophesied event. That event began the church, the body of Christ, the dispensation of grace, God's current program to save Gentiles. One day soon, Jesus will again return in the clouds to rapture the church, the body of Christ. That also will be an unprophesied event. Nowhere in Old Testament prophecy are these two appearances of Jesus coming in the air. According to Zechariah and the two angels present at Jesus' ascension, His next prophesied appearance will be at the Mount of Olives, precisely from where He departed.

The rapture is not part of the prophesied "first resurrection," the resurrection of the just. It is a mystery resurrection specific to the dispensation of grace.

80

Prophecy is for Israel. The mystery is for the body of Christ. You must rightly divide mystery from prophecy, or else you will be confused about coming events.

Satan's Final Deception

"And when the thousand years are expired, Satan shall be loosed out of his prison," - Revelation 20:7

The end of the thousand years sees Satan's release from the bottomless pit, but for what reason? During the Millennial Kingdom, many people are born. They live in a paradise-like environment with no temptation of evil, with Satan chained in the bottomless pit. Those people must endure temptation as all others before them.

Satan's release from the pit will subject all people born during the Millennial Reign of Christ to the temptations of evil.

"And shall go out to deceive the nations which are in the four quarters of the earth, Gog and Magog, to gather them together to battle: the number of whom is as the sand of the sea. And they went up on the breadth of the earth, and compassed the camp of the saints about, and the beloved city: and fire came down from God out of heaven, and devoured them. And the devil that deceived them was cast into the lake of fire and brimstone, where the beast and the false prophet are, and shall be tormented day and night for ever and ever." - Revelation 20:8–10

Satan gathers rebels from Gog and Magog, Asia Minor, Eastern Europe, and southern Russia to make war against God's saints. God quickly disposes of this rabble. Consumed by fire, they are cast into hell to await the final judgment.

God is done with Satan. Evil has no further purpose. Satan joins the beast and the false prophet in the lake of fire. The unholy trinity, together at last, tormented by fire forever and ever.

The Final Judgment

"And I saw a **great white throne**, and him that sat on it, from whose face the earth and the heaven fled away; and there was found no place for them. And I saw **the dead**, small and great, stand before God; and the books were opened: and another book was opened, which is the book of life: and the dead were judged out of those things which were written in the books, **according to their works**. And the sea gave up the dead which were in it; and **death and hell delivered up the dead** which were in them: and they were judged every man according to their **works**. And **death and hell were cast into the lake of fire**. This is the **second death**. And **whosoever was not found written in the book of life was cast into the lake of fire**." - Revelation 20:11–15

The Great White Throne Judgment. I've heard many pastors and teachers claim that everyone will be there to give an account of their lives. Is that true? Here are those that will NOT be there for judgment.

1. Those martyred during the Tribulation will not be there. "He that hath an ear, let him hear what the Spirit saith unto the churches; He that overcometh shall not be hurt of the second death." - Revelation 2:11

2. The Old Testament saints will not be there as they were part of the "first resurrection," the resurrection of the just.

3 The body of Christ, the church will not be there having been raptured and given glorified bodies.

As faithful believers, these three groups have eternal life. Notice the language from verse 12, "And I saw the dead, small and great, stand before God." These are the lost dead. This event is the "resurrection of the unjust."

"Marvel not at this: for the hour is coming, in the which all that are in the graves shall hear his voice, And shall come forth; they that have done good, unto the **resurrection of life**; and they that have done evil, unto the **resurrection of damnation**." - John 5:28–29

"And have hope toward God, which they themselves also allow, that there shall be a **resurrection of the dead, both of the just and unjust**." - Acts 24:15

Everyone, "all that are in the graves," shall come forth in the resurrection.

1. The resurrection of life (the Just). Also called the "first resurrection." This resurrection includes the Old Testament saints (with the Little Flock) and the Tribulation martyrs. Remember, the rapture resurrection was a mystery, therefore not part of the first resurrection.

2. The resurrection of damnation (the unjust). The resurrection of the lost dead to stand before God at the Great White Throne Judgment.

The judgment of those present is according to their works. If their name is not recorded in the "book of life," they are condemned to the lake of fire. This is called the "second death." What does that mean? The condemned were resurrected and given a new body. That's what resurrection means; raised from the dead and alive in a body. They stand before God in that new body. Once condemned, they die again (the second death), and their soul goes to the lake of fire. I cannot imagine the horror of this event.

Summary.

1. The purpose of the Great White Throne judgment is to judge the lost dead, those throughout history that were never saved.

2. The lost dead are resurrected with new bodies to stand before God in judgment. There they will learn their fate and why.

3. They die a second death losing their new body.

4. Their soul is condemned to the lake of fire for all eternity.

Death and hell are cast into the lake of fire. The curse of death brought forth by Adam's sin is finally gone. Having no further need for hell, God condemns that to the lake of fire also.

This present earth and heaven "fled away." The stage is now prepared for chapter 21.

The Eternal State

"And I saw a **new heaven** and a **new earth**: for the first heaven and the first earth were passed away; and there was no more sea." - Revelation 21:1

Why must there be a new heaven and earth? Sin had rendered this present heaven and earth unacceptable to a holy and pure God. This world, tainted with man's sin, must be replaced. The heavens, also stained with the rebellion of Lucifer and a third of heaven's host must also be replaced.

A new heaven and earth prophesied by Isaiah.

"For, behold, I create **new heavens** and a **new earth**: and the former shall not be remembered, nor come into mind." - Isaiah 65:17

Everything is new, even Jerusalem.

"And I John saw the holy city, **new Jerusalem**, coming down from God out of heaven, prepared as a bride adorned for her husband. And I heard a great voice out of heaven saying, Behold, the tabernacle of God is with men, and he will dwell with them, and they shall be his people, and God himself shall be with them, and be their God. And God shall **wipe away all tears** from their eyes; and there shall be **no more death, neither sorrow, nor crying, neither shall there be any more pain: for the former things are passed away.**" - Revelation 21:2-4

We have entered the eternal state. The seven thousand years human experiment is complete. God has accomplished his redemptive plan for sinful humanity. The former things of this earth are gone, including death.

"And he that sat upon the throne said, Behold, I make all things new. And he said unto me, Write: for these words are true and faithful." - Revelation 21:5

God makes all things new. All the old will be destroyed and replaced by the perfect.

Then John gets a tour of the New Jerusalem.

"And he carried me away in the spirit to a great and high mountain, and shewed me that great city, the holy **Jerusalem**, descending out of heaven from God, Having the glory of God: and her light was like unto a stone most precious, even like a jasper stone, clear as crystal; And had a wall great and high, and had twelve gates, and at the gates twelve angels, and names written thereon, which are **the names of the twelve tribes of the children of Israel**:" - Revelation 21:10-12

The names over the twelve gates are the names of the twelve tribes of Israel.

"And the wall of the city had **twelve foundations**, and in them the names of the **twelve apostles of the Lamb**." - Revelation 21:14

The names of the twelve foundations are Jesus' twelve apostles.

The New Jerusalem is enormous, "twelve thousand furlongs," or 1500 miles on each side and 1500 miles high. That would cover half of the United States, from New York City to Cheyenne, Wyoming, and Maine to central Florida. The remainder of chapter 21 discloses much detail about the New Jerusalem.

Chapter 22 speaks of the "river of the water of life" and the "tree of life."

John repeats the urgency from chapter 1.

"Behold, I come quickly: blessed is he that keepeth the sayings of the prophecy of this book." - Revelation 22:7

"And, behold, I come quickly; and my reward is with me, to give every man according as his **work** shall be. ... Blessed are they that do his **commandments**, that they may have right to the tree of life, and may enter in through the gates into the city." - Revelation 22:12, 14

Here again, we read about works and keeping the commandments. Indications that the Law of Moses is in operation.

"I Jesus have sent mine angel to testify unto you these things in the **churches**. I am the root and the offspring of **David**, and the bright and morning star." - Revelation 22:16

Previously, I noted that the churches in chapters 2 and 3 are law-keeping assemblies of Jews, not grace churches. Jesus also describes Himself as the "root and the offspring of David," an entirely Jewish declarative.

Conclusion

The crux of the issue is this. Do chapters 2 & 3, the letters to the seven churches, apply to the Body of Christ? No, they do not. Chapters 2 & 3 apply to churches, assemblies of Jewish believers in Jesus their Messiah, during the Tribulation. They do not apply to us today.

As you continue your study of the books of Hebrews thru Revelation, read them from the mindset of a Jew going through the 7-year Tribulation. That will bring much clarity to your understanding of scripture. The contradictions between John's writings and Paul's epistles will disappear as you discover the two different audiences to whom they are writing. John is an apostle to Israel. Paul is the apostle to the Body of Christ.

Answer to the fundamental questions.

1.   Who is speaking? In the Hebrew epistles of Hebrews thru Revelation, the primary voice is the Holy Spirit speaking through Peter, James, and John, apostles to Israel, the Jews.

2.   Who is the intended audience? Israel, the Jews, not the Body of Christ.

3.   What is the timeframe or setting? The only remaining timeframe for these books is the 7-year Tribulation, wherein God turns His attention back to Israel to fulfill the last-days prophecy.

Thank you and God Bless!

Paul Felter

~ The End ~

Made in the USA
Columbia, SC
09 November 2023

25780291R00052